"*The Giver and the Gift* comp⌐ █████ about fundraising."

"I recommend this book for its au █████

"I found the book fresh, clear, and extremely helpful."
—Denny Rydberg, president, Young Life

"Peter and David's relationship honors the idea that each giver should decide in his or her own heart what to give."
—Brad Formsma, creator, Ilikegiving.com; author, *I Like Giving*

"David and Peter have addressed the donor-fundraiser relationship in an unusual and insightful way."
—Greg Brenneman, CEO, CCMP Capital; former chairman, Burger King and Continental Airlines

"This book will help you rediscover the joy of generosity."
—David Wills, president, National Christian Foundation; coauthor, *Investing in God's Business* and *Family.Money.*

"Peter Greer and David Weekley lucidly demonstrate that fundraising and giving are primarily about partnership."
—Dennis Hollinger, president, Gordon-Conwell Theological Seminary; Coleman M. Mockler Distinguished Professor of Christian Ethics

"Peter and David's powerful stories and keen insight shine light on the partnership God intends between the gift and the giver."
—Lance Wood, partner, PricewaterhouseCoopers

"This book is certain to inspire greater generosity."
— Jeff Rutt, founder and CEO, Keystone Custom Homes; founder, HOPE International

"The truth in this book is enlightening, and I sincerely believe it needs to be read by all nonprofit leaders, development staff, and donors."
—Greg Murtha, chief relationship officer, iDonate

THE
GIVER
AND THE
GIFT

PRINCIPLES *of* KINGDOM
FUNDRAISING

PETER GREER *and*
DAVID WEEKLEY

BETHANYHOUSE
a division of Baker Publishing Group
Minneapolis, Minnesota

Published by Bethany House Publishers
11400 Hampshire Avenue South
Bloomington, Minnesota 55438
www.bethanyhouse.com

Bethany House Publishers is a division of
Baker Publishing Group, Grand Rapids, Michigan

Printed in the United States of America

Library of Congress Cataloging-in-Publication Data
Greer, Peter.
    The giver and the gift : principles of kingdom fundraising / Peter Greer and
David Weekley.
        pages cm
    Summary: "Presents an approach to fundraising that benefits the donor and
the receiver and that is founded on generous relationships that value the giver and
the gift"— Provided by publisher.
    ISBN 978-0-7642-1774-6 (pbk. : alk. paper)
    1. Church fund raising. 2. Church finance. 3. Christian giving. I. Title.
BV772.5.G74 2015
254′.8—dc23   2015025268

Cover design by LOOK Design Studio

Authors are represented by Wolgemuth and Associates.

15   16   17   18   19   20   21   7   6   5   4   3   2   1

Dedicated to Terry Looper and Rusty Walter
for their friendship and generosity.

A cord of three strands is not easily broken.
Ecclesiastes 4:12 HCSB

Books by Peter Greer

The Giver and the Gift
(coauthored by David Weekley)

40/40 Vision
(coauthored by Greg Lafferty)

Mission Drift
(coauthored by Chris Horst with Anna Haggard)

The Spiritual Danger of Doing Good
(with Anna Haggard)

Entrepreneurship for Human Flourishing
(coauthored by Chris Horst)

Watching Seeds Grow
(coauthored by Keith Greer)

Mommy's Heart Went Pop!
(coauthored by Christina Kyllonen)

The Poor Will Be Glad
(coauthored by Phil Smith)

Contents

Foreword by Fred Smith   9

Introduction   11

Part I: The Gift   15

1. Christ-Centered, Not Me-Centered   25

2. Listen First, Speak Second   28

3. Generous, Not Greedy   32

4. Clarity, Not Ambiguity   35

5. Real, Not Rose-Colored   38

6. Patient, Not Overambitious   42

7. Confident, Not Arrogant   45

8. Long-Term, Not Short-Lived   48

9. Grateful, Not Entitled   51

10. Represents, Not Uses   54

Part II: The Giver   59

11. Stewardship, Not Ownership   65

12. Heads, Not Just Hearts   68

13. Mission Minded, Not Manipulative   72

14. Partnership, Not Dependency   75

15. Transformational Giving, Not Just Informed
    Philanthropy   78

16. Spirit-Led, Not Overly Structured   82

17. Anonymous or Named?   85

18. The Kids or the Kingdom?   88

19. For Forever or For Now?   91

20. Together, Not Alone   94

   Conclusion   97

   Acknowledgments   99

   Appendix 1: David Weekley Family Foundation's
   International Giving Summary   101

   Notes   107

   About the Authors   110

FOREWORD

Several years ago, I wrote a review for a book on fundraising that was never published. I took issue with one of the assumptions about relationships with donors. The author started from the premise that wealthy donors are rich in possessions but poor in spirit, and the role of the fundraiser is to minister to their hurts and needs. There was no mention of the opportunity to learn from the experience and competence of donors, nor of the possibility that not all donors might need another ministry friend to come alongside them just then.

The formulaic relationship described in that book does not at all reflect the dynamic, honest, and sincere bond forged by Peter Greer and David Weekley. What they have found in each other's company is a shared respect for their different strengths and perspectives. The genuine friendship and mutuality that they have is rare between peers but almost nonexistent between major donors and ministry leaders. The pressure for the leader to conform to donor expectations or for the donor to control the programs of the ministry is ever-present, and learning how David and Peter have managed to resist that pattern is one of the rewards of reading this book. Over time, they have learned to grow each other and not be content with a merely transactional relationship.

Yes, there are plenty of very practical ideas and issues addressed in this book, but for me, the extraordinary relationship they have formed based on trust is what is truly remarkable. When I first worked with Bob Buford at Leadership Network, we sat down and said, "What can we expect of each other?" We wrote down several things and would review them periodically to make sure our relationship stayed healthy. We wanted to be partners in the work that was larger than either of us. That is what David and Peter have done in their own way. They are committed to accomplishing a common purpose, and they each bring different gifts to the work.

Among all the other things you will get from this book I would hope when you are finished you will be motivated to find someone with whom you can have a similar relationship of trust, friendship, and mutual respect. Whether you are a donor or a ministry leader, there could be nothing more satisfying than being engaged in work that is purposeful with a partner whose life and strengths you value and from whom you can learn.

Fred Smith
President of The Gathering

INTRODUCTION

PETER GREER & DAVID WEEKLEY

On December 5, 1835, a young preacher fell to his knees in prayer after reading a simple statement: "Open thy mouth wide, and I will fill it."[1] To George Mueller, these words were the promise of something he had long dreamed of building: an orphanage in his underserved English neighborhood. With faith in God's promised blessing, he boldly petitioned the Lord for an orphanage house, staff, furniture, children's clothing, and finances. He spoke to *no one else* about his requests.

In the days and months that followed, Mueller received everything that he prayed for in full. Without being asked, one couple donated all of their personal furniture for the orphanage and volunteered as unsalaried orphan caretakers. Another couple provided fabric and clothes for the children. Still others promised weekly gifts or large one-time donations. Mueller's answered prayer was the start of a lifelong commitment to faith in God's provision.

Just a few years later, Hudson Taylor was preparing to move from England to China, where he would eventually found the China Inland Mission and raise over $4 million (more than $118 million in today's valuation). In contrast to Mueller's method of silent prayer,

Taylor often spent large amounts of time speaking to potential donors about ministry needs.

From Mueller and Taylor's experience in the 1800s to today, philanthropy has grown into a multi-billion dollar industry, grossing over $330 billion each year in the U.S.[2]

What is the "right way" to go about fundraising today? Is it to silently pray and wait, like Mueller? Is it to actively seek new opportunities to share the message, like Taylor? Or is it something else entirely?

Today, most nonprofit staff and boards spend considerable time praying, thinking, planning, and fretting about fundraising. More than virtually any other subject, raising the annual budget is a regular focus and concern.

Likewise, many donors meet with peer groups, attend conferences, and read books to discuss generosity and high-impact philanthropy. The desire is to help without hurting and ensure our charity does not turn toxic.[3]

Bur rarely is there a place for organizational leaders *and* donors to join in thoughtful conversation about fundraising and generosity. Typically, books and conferences target *either* donors or fundraisers; there are few places for both to engage in honest discussion and learn from the others' perspective.

Our hope is that this simple book provides a safe place for this type of conversation.

Our friendship started after David returned from a trip to Rwanda and began considering if and how he should engage in international philanthropy. Since Peter had recently returned from living in Rwanda, we connected on a phone call, which was followed by a brief meeting in Houston, which was followed by a trip together to the Dominican Republic, which was followed by a trip to Rwanda and Burundi, which was followed by a decade of conversation and partnership.

We chose to write this book together because we believe supporters and organizational leaders are called into relationship with one another. We believe everyone has something to give and something to learn. We believe there is a different way to think about a Kingdom approach to fundraising. And we are excited to imagine the impact of unleashed generosity through mutually encouraging partnerships.

The first half of this book, "The Gift," is written from Peter's perspective as a ministry leader. The second half, "The Giver," is written from David's viewpoint as a donor. Although we write from an individual, first-person perspective, our thoughts have been sharpened, challenged, and impacted by our friendship. Our hope is that the principles in this book have relevance for anyone involved in raising or donating funds for Christian causes.

Join us as we consider how to invest, support, partner, and serve together in seeing "Thy Kingdom come, on earth as it is in heaven."[4]

PART 1

THE
GIFT

PETER GREER

Traveling from Boston to Lancaster, Pennsylvania, for my final interview, I was thrilled at the prospect of joining HOPE International. With a clear identity and compelling mission, I believed this was an organization poised for growth.

Addressing the board of directors, I enthusiastically presented my assessment of the organization's strengths, weaknesses, opportunities, and threats through a carefully scripted presentation I'd spent weeks rehearsing.

And then the interview questions began. Most of them I'd anticipated and felt prepared to answer.

"Where do you see the organization in five years?"

"Who are three people who had the most significant influence on you and why?"

"What criteria would you use to assess potential expansion opportunities?"

Then Tom, one of the board members, asked, "We've been speaking primarily about our operations, but do you have any experience fundraising?"

Fundraising?

A hush fell over the room as my eyes widened. Until that point, I'd somehow missed the critical detail that fundraising was an important component of the role for which I was interviewing.

"Well, I've managed some technical grants, . . . and I have raised funds when I went on a church mission trip in high school. . . ." I stammered.

Pausing, I realized the more direct answer to Tom's question.

"No, I've never done any significant fundraising."

I will forever be deeply grateful that despite my lack of knowledge or experience, the board still offered me a role—but they gave me a clear assignment along with my job offer.

"In the next three months, we would like you to raise your annual salary."

Gulp.

I was wildly enthusiastic about every part of my new role—except fundraising.

Where would I even begin?

After moving with my wife to Pennsylvania and fully committing to the organization, I discovered an alarming fact: Our organization's bank account was dangerously low, and we had already tapped into our emergency line of credit.

Our passion for the mission became overshadowed by the reality that without funding, it would be impossible to accomplish any of the organization's objectives.

With a clear vision and a growing program, we had a road map and a car—but little gas in the tank. While our founder had generously covered the majority of the organization's expenses since its inception, we needed to broaden our base of support. And we needed to act quickly.

With nervous excitement, I discovered a foundation that, on paper, seemed like it would have an interest in our Christ-centered microfinance model. Hopping in my car with a stack of brochures and a stomach full of butterflies, I drove to my first potential major donor meeting.

Arriving in Richmond at a posh colonial office complex, I entered with sweaty palms and a wildly beating heart. Seated at a round wooden table with Adrianne, I nervously began to verbally vomit our mission, key objectives, and plans for the future.

Adrianne listened. She asked thoughtful questions. But she made it clear it was unlikely the foundation would ever give to HOPE. They simply had other priorities in other parts of the world.

My heart sank.

However, Adrianne didn't let me leave that meeting empty handed. Sensing my trepidation in this first feeble fundraising effort, she understood that more than a check, what I needed was a change in perspective.

She spoke about fundraising in terms of partnership. Then she handed me a copy of Henri Nouwen's *The Spirituality of Fundraising*. Our conversation began a slow process of radically redesigning how I view fundraising.

It wasn't until I started reading Nouwen's book that I recognized that I had an Oliver Twist perspective of fundraising. Subconsciously, I believed that there are people with money and power, and there are others with their heads down and hands up, timidly asking for "just a little more" porridge.

Adrianne understood that this perspective did a gross disservice to the donors I would be interacting with, to the organization I represented, and to God, who owned all of the resources. She graciously shared with me that my idea of fundraising had to be fundamentally altered.

Walking out of this meeting, my mind was spinning with questions:

What if giving, at its core, is a spiritual exercise?

What if generosity is a necessary part of every single discipleship journey?

What if fundraising has the potential to be good for the giver, and not just the receiver?

What if fundraising is about love and service, and not just "What's in it for me?"

What if everything I've ever thought about fundraising is wrong?

And last, but feeling most urgent, . . . *What if I'm a failure?*

Several months later, I traveled to the Dominican Republic with David Weekley and a small group of successful entrepreneurs from Texas. We were on a trip to observe Christ-centered microfinance through our partnership with Esperanza International. As we drove through winding, dusty roads amid sugarcane fields, we talked about strategic planning and building an organization. I soaked up their wisdom like a sponge.

On the plane ride home, David commented, "Peter, we've spent time together visiting the program and talking about the future. I like what I see. But you have not talked at all about the needs and opportunities to come alongside you in this ministry or invited me to participate." Smiling, he added, "We're about to land—don't you want to ask for something?"

Though I was energized by the programmatic aspects of my role, I was uncomfortable, awkward, and ill-prepared for anything having to do with fundraising. So I avoided it completely with David and virtually everyone else.

David's words were still fresh in my mind when we landed back in Texas. As we got ready to say our goodbyes, one of the trip participants, Terry, pulled me aside and warmly said, "Thank you, Peter."

Baffled, I remember thinking, *Why in the world is he thanking me?*

Terry continued, "I don't have the flexibility to travel around the world investing in Kingdom impact. But I've been blessed with resources, and you're an essential partner in using those resources for God's glory."

He concluded, "I can't do what God has called me to do without you."

He needed *me* in order to do what God had called *him* to do?

Without knowing it, Terry erased my Oliver Twist perspective of fundraising. He upended my perception of the power dynamics, revealing fundraising as a partnership in which both the giver and the receiver mutually need each other. No longer was I sheepishly holding out my empty hands, begging for just enough to get by. Rather, I was a business partner, or as the apostle Paul wrote, part of a "partnership in the gospel."[1]

Along with Adrianne, Terry introduced me to a new concept: fundraising as a Kingdom partnership. And this perspective has changed everything about how our team and I think about raising funds.

In Kingdom fundraising, we acknowledge that together we can accomplish something far greater than we could ever accomplish alone. It's a collaboration in which both parties have something to give and something to receive. It's a spiritual exercise, rooted in relationship, for the advancement of Christ's Kingdom. It's about something much bigger and more important than meeting an annual budget.

And it can be a whole lot more fun than I ever imagined.

Something's Wrong

A 2008 Harvard study confirmed that giving is good for you. Generous people are happier than those who spend their resources primarily on themselves.[2]

Social psychologist Liz Dunn conducted a study that examined cortisol levels in response to giving away money. Cortisol, often known as "the stress hormone," exists in higher levels when responding to stress or trauma. In Dunn's experiment, the more money people kept for themselves, the higher their cortisol levels were.[3]

Similarly, researchers from the University of Buffalo found that there was a correlation between giving and longer life.[4]

Long before this research, truths of generosity's benefits were plainly etched in Scripture. Jesus reminds us that it is "more blessed to give than to receive,"[5] and Solomon's wisdom in Proverbs tells us that "a generous person will prosper; whoever refreshes others will be refreshed."[6]

Based on the abundance of scriptural and scientific research on the benefits of giving, you'd think that fundraising would be a highly celebrated and meaningful career, right?

Yet the data suggests something different.

The average tenure of a professional fundraiser is around sixteen months,[7] and as many as one in four development directors expect to leave the entire *field* of development within two years.[8]

Even hiring fundraisers is a serious challenge. In a recent study, 46 percent of organizations with an open development director position reported a vacancy length of over six months. And 53 percent of executives reported the candidates who applied during that time were underqualified.[9]

When it comes to fundraising, many would prefer the proverbial root canal to asking someone else to support a cause they passionately care about.

So what's the problem?

Over lunch in Atlanta, former NFL player and philanthropist Todd Peterson bluntly summarized, "There are too many bad fundraisers trying to raise money in the wrong way." Poor practices are giving the entire sector a bad name. He continued by explaining how many fundraisers are looking for transactions rather than desiring transformational relationships.

And this reputation is not altogether incorrect—much of modern fundraising really is distasteful. For example, at a development conference, one veteran fundraiser advised using reverse psychology to manipulate people into giving. She will say to potential donors, "Because the population we're serving is difficult, this probably isn't the sort of cause you'd want to be involved in."

She reasons that when you tell someone they can't have something, they will want it.

Manipulation is not just the realm of high pressure time-share sales pitches; that same level of stressful experience is also commonly found in fundraising.

Due to a very long line of manipulative and unhelpful practices, organizations have sought ways to avoid the negative stereotypes that come with the job. Many have even gone so far as to change the job title of fundraisers. At the 2013 annual meeting of the National

Association of Fundraisers, one group of professionals identified twenty-eight alternatives to the position name, including:

Development Representative

Advancement Officer

Major Gifts Officer

Head of Resource Mobilization

Director of Strategic Alliances

Director of Philanthropy

Chief Storyteller

Head Campaigner

And the list goes on and on.

The reason for all the creative titles is obvious. Some (falsely) think that if they change their titles, donors will be more willing to meet with them. But it's only a matter of time before someone else damages the revised term and leaders have to seek a new expression.

Instead of changing titles, it's time to change our approach and rediscover an alternative perspective on fundraising—one that, at its core, is focused on the Kingdom and rooted in relationships. In this paradigm, we seek to simply love God and love our neighbor. It's more about our attitude and motivation than new techniques.

In this little book, we want to share ten ways to approach fundraising with a Kingdom perspective:

1. Christ-Centered, Not Me-Centered

2. Listen First, Speak Second

3. Generous, Not Greedy

4. Clarity, Not Ambiguity

5. Real, Not Rose-Colored
6. Patient, Not Overambitious
7. Confident, Not Arrogant
8. Long-Term, Not Short-Lived
9. Grateful, Not Entitled
10. Represents, Not Uses

Following this section, David Weekley shares his perspective on ways to practice effective philanthropy from a donor's viewpoint:

11. Stewardship, Not Ownership
12. Heads, Not Just Hearts
13. Mission Minded, Not Manipulative
14. Partnership, Not Dependency
15. Transformational Giving, Not Just Informed Philanthropy
16. Spirit-Led, Not Overly Structured
17. Anonymous or Named?
18. The Kids or the Kingdom?
19. For Forever or For Now?
20. Together, Not Alone

We hope these side-by-side perspectives might enhance meaningful conversation between the giver and the organization receiving the gift, increasing joy for both and resulting in a flood of high-impact partnerships.

As the apostle Paul wrote to the Corinthian church thousands of years ago, together may we all learn to "excel in this grace of giving."[10]

1

CHRIST-CENTERED, NOT ME-CENTERED

Christ is either Lord of all, or He is not Lord at all.
—Hudson Taylor

When Chris Crane, a member of my board, and I stepped into a high-end office complex in San Diego, I was expecting to race past the fountains and statues in search of our meeting place. Instead, I discovered that our first stop was in the lobby, where Chris bowed his head and asked me to join him in prayer.

I listened as he thanked the Lord for the opportunity to meet with this group of potential donors. He prayed for wisdom to know when to speak and what to say. He asked that we would be an encouragement, and he gave glory to God for whatever would be accomplished.

"God, we want to listen to you and follow your guidance," Chris said.

Then he paused.

I joined him in the silence, realizing Chris was intentionally, expectantly listening for the Lord's response. After a couple of minutes, he said, "Amen," and we headed to the elevator and up to the conference room.

Chris understood that at its core, fundraising is spiritual. Doing it well means listening for the Holy Spirit's guidance. If that meant presenting a specific giving opportunity, we were ready. If it meant simply listening, we were ready. If it meant connecting the donor to a different organization that was better aligned with what God had impressed upon their hearts, we were ready.

Chris's highest goal was not to raise funds for an organization; it was to follow the Spirit's leading.

Christ's Kingdom is the true aim; money is a vehicle, not the ultimate objective. Standing in the San Diego lobby that day, I had a profound sense that we were about our Father's business, not the business of any one organization.

No matter the circumstance, Jesus always acknowledged the need to depend on His Father's leading. When the Pharisees criticized Him for healing a sick man on the Sabbath, He reminded them of the Father's authority: "Very truly I tell you, the Son can do nothing by himself; he can do only what he sees his Father doing, because whatever the Father does the Son also does."[1]

When we have a Kingdom approach to fundraising, we patiently wait for God to lead. All resources belong to Him. And He is infinitely more interested in helping His people than we are, so we look to Him to point us to His resources that He wants to use.

Above all, we focus on the Kingdom. We listen to God's leading. And we know there is a higher good that goes far beyond any personal or organizational goals.

DISCUSSION QUESTIONS

- Donors have long been plagued by fundraisers who have no ability to see beyond their personal agenda. Imagine the difference in someone who is truly focused on building the Kingdom.

- How might you spend time asking the Lord to go before you and move in the hearts of those you're about to talk to?

2

LISTEN FIRST, SPEAK SECOND

There is a difference between listening and waiting for your turn to speak.

—Simon Sinek

After my episode of verbal vomiting with Adrianne in Richmond a few years ago, I now try to be much quicker to listen and slower to speak. But listening, I've discovered, is something of a rare skill.

More than three decades ago, American philosopher Mortimer Adler wrote:

Is anyone anywhere taught how to listen? How utterly amazing is the general assumption that the ability to listen well is a natural gift for which no training is required. How extraordinary is the fact that no effort is made anywhere in the whole educational process to help individuals learn how to listen well.[1]

The human brain thinks somewhere between 1,000 and 3,000 words per minute but listens at a much slower rate of between 125 and 250 words per minute.[2] The odds are not in our favor when it comes to listening.

We need to breathe deeply as we focus on what's said.

When done right, active listening can transform relationships. In the same way that our love for friends and family motivates us to listen closely to them, it's genuine care that inspires us to really listen to supporters when they share their stories. It's when we listen that we have open ears to hear their needs and learn from their experiences. And it's then that we're enabled to serve in a whole new way.

When a couple mentioned that they wanted to expose their children to international ministries, we helped organize an experience where they visited five ministries in one week.

When another donor shared that he had little interest in funding day-to-day operations, we were able to present specific projects and capital expenses that matched his interests.

Active listening, coupled with a Kingdom approach, also means that there are times we connect supporters to other organizations that better align with their passions or calling.

One example was when a supporter mentioned his decision to begin focusing his international philanthropy on Guatemala, a country where we were not operating. After researching organizations in Guatemala, we discovered another excellent Christ-centered organization operating there that aligned with his interests. We made an introduction, essentially ending his support for us, but that introduction began a significant new level of support for the other organization.

Even though introductions like this may result in less direct funding for our organization, they are Kingdom successes.

When we listen well and choose an attitude of abundance over an attitude of scarcity, we can let go of our unhealthy white-knuckle grasp on any relationship or resource.

Listening also guides how we pray. When a situation with children brought unexpected challenges to a donor, our global staff was able to pray for and support our friends. Our ministry then becomes twofold: We reach out to families around the world as well as to supporters.

While such gestures of listening may seem commonplace, they are—perhaps because of less than ideal practices—unusual in fundraising. Raising the bar means refusing to see fundraising as a transaction, but rather as a relationship. And deepening relationships means spending far more time listening than speaking.

Listening well also involves asking insightful questions that will teach us about supporters' interests.

What are their passions? Why are they interested in the organization? How do they wish to involve their family in philanthropy? What experiences impacted the way they approach giving? What was their most meaningful gift? When have they been frustrated with organizations? Where might their passions overlap with the organization's objectives?

Intentional listening may be a lost art, but it's one that everyone involved in Kingdom fundraising needs to rediscover. And in listening, we begin to understand what God is doing in their lives and how we might be a part of advancing that significant work.

DISCUSSION QUESTIONS

- Do you start every meeting with questions to better understand supporters' passions?

- Have you listened well to try to understand what God is doing in their lives?

- What proportion of time do you spend speaking versus listening?

3

Generous, Not Greedy

No one has ever become poor by giving.
—Anne Frank

The most convincing salespeople are those who have purchased the very product they're selling. Likewise, the most convincing fundraisers are those who are personally invested in the organization they represent.

Why should we ask anyone else to do what we haven't done ourselves? It was an encouragement when our finance team informed me that, unsolicited, 80 percent of our team who had been on staff for more than two years were financially contributing to our organization.

A generous fundraiser always devotes time and resources to the cause.

But a generous fundraiser also seeks to be generous with the supporters. Is it the donor's birthday or anniversary? Mail a card. New child or grandchild in the family? Let them know you're rejoicing with them. Celebratory occasions are a great place to build relationships, but somber times are perhaps an even more important opportunity to show care.

After a longtime donor had a family tragedy, our staff sent him a sympathy card. When Chris Horst, HOPE's vice president of development, chatted with him about it, the normally reserved, stoic donor choked up as he considered the thoughtfulness of the team.

"He was without words to explain how it felt that a group of people whom he has never met were willing to take a few minutes to express their condolences," Chris shared.

Let's be clear, though: A condolence note is not a tactic for giving. It is not something to be crossed off a checklist, and it certainly is not a marketing strategy.

It is simply an expression of love. It's what people do in real relationships. And it's how the body of Christ responds to pain.

We serve a God of generosity, and we want to be people who emulate our Savior. Jesus was always giving, always serving, even choosing to wash the filthy feet of His disciples. Even Christ's first recorded miracle was somewhat menial: He turned water into wine for a wedding feast. He chose to first care about what mattered to the people He loved in the place where He was.

When we model Christ's generosity, it has a tendency to spread. Generous fundraisers often spark generous donors, who inspire generous staff around the world.

Timothy, a field coordinator in Rwanda, experienced this first-hand when he was in a near-fatal accident. As he recovered in the hospital, members of the four hundred savings groups under his direction caught wind of the situation. Without hesitation, each of them began to save an additional 15–20 cents each meeting. The outcome was a total of three million Rwandan Francs, the equivalent of $5,000, to put toward Timothy's medical expenses. Most of these hard-working individuals earn less than $1.50 a day. Yet with collaboration fueled by generosity, they were able to produce a gift of magnitude and impact.

In a Kingdom perspective on fundraising, *everyone* is invited to be a giver as we live generously in response to the resounding grace we've received.

DISCUSSION QUESTIONS

- Do you know supporters' interests, hobbies, and passions?

- Before asking others to give, have you financially supported the cause yourself?

4

CLARITY, NOT AMBIGUITY

The greatest beauty always lies in the greatest clarity.
—Gotthold Ephraim Lessing

When I first joined HOPE, we operated in Ukraine and China and were preparing to launch operations in the Democratic Republic of Congo. As I met with potential supporters, I spoke about the model we had developed in Ukraine, but I also shared about all we were hoping to accomplish in our new context. This required clear goals with distinctly articulated outcomes.

Annually, I would return to supporters and report progress based on the areas of impact shared the year before. Not only did this keep supporters engaged in their partnership, it also helped me realize that, early on, my ideas were often unrealistic. I had grand plans, but we did not have the organizational capacity to accomplish them in the time frame I anticipated.

Having clear plans and goals provided an important level of organizational accountability, as well as a seriousness about our partnership with supporters.

For a lasting partnership, it is important to have clarity on goals, communicated concisely, and then regular updates on what *actually happened*.

Without goals up front and then clear communication on the results, how will supporters know if our mission is in line with their passions and calling? How else will we know the impact we're having together?

Imagine making an investment in a company, but then experiencing silence. No regular updates on the returns. No clue on the successes or challenges faced by the company. No idea of the current value of your investment.

What is unlikely in investing is surprisingly normal in the world of "investing" in Christian ministries. How many times have you given to individuals going on a trip and yet never really heard what happened while they were away? How many organizations communicated clearly before the gift, but then went silent after it was received?

Clarity on goals and follow-through on results should be normative when experiencing a partnership approach to raising funds. It's the simple things like follow-up emails and "yes" meaning "yes." If you say, "I'll send you additional information on that particular program," actually send the email with the requested information within twenty-four hours. And always be sure to follow up when objectives are—or aren't—achieved.

Just like any investment, it is our responsibility to share the actual outcomes and lessons learned through experience. It's not enough to simply tell a donor where their money *will* go; you also have to come back and tell them where it *went*. It's not enough to just share what you *hope* to accomplish; you also have to share what you *did* accomplish.

Galileo once advised, "Measure what is measurable, and make measurable what is not so."[1] Successful organizations exhibit this motto in their metrics and reporting. They invest in appropriate monitoring and evaluation and are constantly learning.

Even with objectives that are not easily quantifiable, the goal is still to figure out creative ways to go beyond stories. Whether this is done through creative qualitative surveys or quantitative measurement, there often is a way to talk specifically about impact.

For successful collaboration, we need to be clear about what we are trying to accomplish and then be serious about measuring and reporting results.

DISCUSSION QUESTIONS

- What steps are you taking to ensure that your message is clear and measurable?

- Does each supporter see a connection between giving and organizational accomplishments?

5

REAL,
NOT ROSE-COLORED

Honesty is the first chapter in the book of wisdom.
—Thomas Jefferson

While in college, I was invited by our alumni office to represent our school at a college fair for high school students. After a day of meeting with prospective students, another college rep asked me to go to dinner.

I agreed, eager for a conversation about something other than financial aid packages.

Halfway through dinner, the conversation abruptly became awkward.

"What are your financial goals in life?" he asked suddenly. "Would you like to be a millionaire by the time you're thirty?"

You may have encountered this form of subtle multi-level marketing pitch. The meeting purpose is vague. Without fully disclosing their identity, the other person promises that massive wealth awaits you and then unveils a giant pyramid scheme.

The overall sense is that the meeting just isn't real.

Too often in trying to raise funds, we pursue a similar path. We cloud our titles and purposes, attempting to disguise our motives for meeting.

The stereotypical salesman is a classic example of this: He mirrors your statement, even if he has to lie. So if you were just in Disneyland, he would say, "I was just in Disneyland too!"

Others invite affluent individuals to serve on councils or advisory boards without any intention of listening to their advice; it's simply another ploy to get funding.

Why not simply be honest about the need to raise funds for an organization that we believe is having a significant impact? Why not boldly ask for an opportunity to share why we are so passionate about our ministries?

If the goal of a meeting is to present funding opportunities, we should be honest about the intentions of the meeting, giving donors the chance to opt out before we even begin the conversation. Some people will decline meetings, and we can't be offended by that. In a Kingdom fundraising perspective, honesty is indispensable.

Consider how hard it is for donors to trust nonprofits in a world where every nonprofit website has an amazing graphic design and a compelling mission statement. How are givers ever supposed to distinguish fact from fiction? Any organization can look awesome with the right marketing materials. Without spending considerable time in research, donors have a hard time discerning the truth about an organization.

Fundraisers must be the people who uphold honesty and transparency in their relationships. Otherwise, the distrust gap between staff and donors will never close.

A commitment to truth begins with clarity about the purposes of meetings, but continues in being honest with progress. Donors deserve dignity, respect, and truth—and this includes both successes and failures.

We experienced this firsthand at HOPE when we faced significant challenges with our fledgling program in the Democratic Republic of Congo.

After incredible initial success was quickly followed by failure, I was responsible for communicating our subpar performance. It wasn't just the staff with whom we had to share our failings—I knew we needed to share what had happened with some of our key supporters, as well. I had a pit in my stomach as I headed to a luncheon with a group of our largest and most influential supporters.

I felt responsible, and I felt ashamed for letting everyone down: the hardworking entrepreneurs in the DRC, the staff, and the donors.

But after discussing our failures, this group of supporters was incredibly gracious. They wanted to know how we had responded. They wanted to hear what we had learned and what we were doing differently as a result. And then they offered words of encouragement about some of their lowest times and how God used even the failures to teach them lifelong lessons.

Their words reminded me of something that businessman Jim Amos once shared with me: "All we get on the mountaintop is a good view. The real change comes through the hard work of the climb."

As hard as it is to share our shortcomings, I believe humble transparency about our failures points the glory back to God for any good things that we do. I like how Paul phrases it: "Therefore I will *boast* all the more gladly about my weaknesses, so that Christ's power may rest on me."[1]

DISCUSSION QUESTIONS

- Have you been clear about your role and purposes when setting up meetings?

- Have you communicated successes *and* failures?

- Where might you need to be even more candid with supporters?

6

PATIENT,
NOT OVERAMBITIOUS

He that can have patience can have what he will.
—Benjamin Franklin

Early on in my time with HOPE, I met with the leaders of a large, renowned Christian foundation in Tennessee. During the meeting, they listened graciously about our mission but shared their passion for the 10/40 window and media outreach strategies.

Returning to Pennsylvania the next day, our team created a proposal for the foundation, despite the fact that they hadn't extended an invitation to do so. It didn't feel like the right timing or that our mission was perfectly in line with their priorities, but we were behind on our fundraising goals. After sending the proposal, I waited hopefully.

Almost immediately, we received a rather cold decline.

And, truth be told, I wasn't surprised—I had jumped when I should have waited. That was the last time I made an unsolicited ask. Unsolicited proposals are often unwelcome proposals, similar to a door-to-door salesman interrupting the family dinner.

In any sort of sales, timing is key. When we ask, we want to be sure the invitation will be appreciated. As my friend Terry Looper taught me, asking too soon is like asking someone to marry you without knowing if they even like you—and it's uncomfortable for everyone involved.

When my wife, Laurel, and I had our first date rafting down the Nile River in Uganda, I knew she was the woman I wanted to spend the rest of my life with. Unsure if she felt the same way, I did not get down on one knee at the end of the day and ask her to marry me. Rather, I waited until I had a good idea she felt something similar and that chances were fairly high she would say yes. In our situation, that meant waiting seven more weeks (I didn't want to rush into anything) before proposing on my rooftop overlooking Kigali, the capital of Rwanda. A shooting star raced across the sky (seriously). The timing was perfect.

She said yes. And I have been thankful to walk with her ever since.

The point is that we have to wait until we have some sort of reasonable expectation that our invitation for marriage—or a fundraising proposal—will be well received.

If we truly see fundraising as an invitation to the table, we can't expect everyone to be hungry at the same time. A Kingdom-focused fundraiser is less concerned with short-term wins and more concerned with long-term relationships.

Practically, this means we have to have a much longer timeline for measuring success or failure than quarterly. Putting external time pressure on a relationship has the potential to undermine it before it even begins. Rather than letting short-term goals guide the relationship, we should let God's leading and the donor's timeline guide our actions.

Knowing when to ask is always a tricky process. Some people balk when asked for a specific amount; some won't take you seriously until you do. This is another reason why listening is so crucial. Kingdom-focused fundraisers make proposals only after adequate preparation and relationship building. A request for partnership should never take the donor by surprise, or something's been missed in the process.

Again, my experience is that unsolicited requests are a waste of time and money, and generally unappreciated by potential supporters.

If we want to see results, we need to invest time in the process and never let short-term goals sabotage long-term relationships.

DISCUSSION QUESTIONS

- Have you waited patiently for the right opportunity to present partnership opportunities?

- What has happened when you haven't waited?

- What has happened when you have?

7

CONFIDENT,
NOT ARROGANT

Faith is to believe what you do not see; the reward of
this faith is to see what you believe.

—St. Augustine

On the top floor of a Houston high-rise, I sat across from a senior
executive of a global oil and gas corporation. He led the company's
charitable giving.

For over two years, we had cultivated this relationship. Late into
many evenings, HOPE International staff members wrote reports
to meet their deadlines. We even sent a field director to visit their
London office—offering an inside glimpse of our microenterprise
programs in sub-Saharan Africa. Until now, their financial support
had been helpful, but relatively small scale.

But that could change. The executive articulated that he'd caught our vision. He wanted to help us provide business training, create savings accounts, and give small-business loans to many more under-resourced entrepreneurs in some of the most challenging countries in the world.

Rising from his seat, he said, "There is just one remaining issue." He paused. I held my breath.

"We are a publicly traded company and we cannot fund organizations that are so overtly faith based."

If our organization would tone down our Christian mission, his foundation would champion our cause. And we weren't talking pennies. They were ready to write a very large check. With their support, we could help many families throughout Africa and Asia pursue their dreams. Thousands—perhaps hundreds of thousands—more individuals could break the cycle of poverty.

I did not give an immediate response. Instead, I thanked him for the offer and headed to the airport.

I didn't know what to do.

Everything in me wanted to make this work. We were friends. The company possessed extraordinary giving potential. I respected its leaders. And we were cash strapped.

Several of our board members initially encouraged us to explore a creative way to develop this partnership. For the good of our mission, couldn't we just "tone down" our Christian identity?[1]

Realizing that our mission was not just economic development, we turned down the funding and reexamined our direction. While we believe strongly in microfinance, Christ is at the core of who we are—and that's something we are unwilling to compromise. From that point on, we have learned to clearly and humbly describe who we are—and to know our mission will not resonate with all foundations or philanthropists.

Kingdom-focused fundraisers have the courage and confidence to decline funding opportunities that might pull an organization off mission. They are not arrogant, but they understand that, for the best of both the donors and the organization, funding needs to be in line with the full mission.

For fundraisers, confidence in the mission can sometimes slip into organizational arrogance where the individual has an inability to see anything beyond their own agenda and mission. In a recent meeting, HOPE's vice president of development, Chris Horst, sat down with a fundraiser from a noteworthy organization who had one and only one purpose during the conversation: "convincing me that his ministry was the crème de la crème," as Chris put it. "For over 90 percent of the meeting, I sat and listened as he lauded the exploits of his mission."

It's not an uncommon experience. And it's one I've had many times.

As Chris shared, "Subtly, however, this approach crosses the line from enthusiasm to arrogance, communicating to me and others: What you are involved in is less important than what I am involved in. Where God has you matters less than where God has me."

This approach exposes a far too narrow view of the Kingdom of God. Let's humbly stand tall, explain our mission with confidence, and celebrate the successes of any organization doing important work.

DISCUSSION QUESTIONS

- If you were to face a situation where you needed to turn down a financial partnership, how would you handle it?

- What tone would you use, and what response would you give that communicated love and confidence, not arrogance?

8

LONG-TERM,
NOT SHORT-LIVED

If you read history you will find that the Christians who
did most for the present world were precisely those who
thought most of the next.

—C. S. Lewis

The job of a fundraiser isn't to change hearts. It is simply to have
the sensitivity in our spirit to join the work that God is already
doing. Learning to follow His leading means keeping a long-term
focus.

There was a potential supporter I met with twice a year for eight
years. We had explored partnership, but his interests were focused
domestically.

It was clear, though, that he was still interested in learning more about our organization. After eight years, he asked for a proposal and responded with a check, along with a challenge: "Make me believe we can help internationally without hurting." Hearing stories of international projects gone awry, he had reasons to be concerned, yet he also sensed a call to become more engaged internationally.

At its heart, a partnership isn't just about the money—it's also about the relationship. Oftentimes, the longer the relationship, the more meaningful it becomes.

The single most important indicator of the health of a development team is not the annual budget, but rather the attrition rate. Of the people who supported you in the past, how many continue with you the following year? And even when people no longer support you, do you still find ways to stay in relationship?

Several years ago, one of our faithful donors went bankrupt. It was clear that it would be a very long time before he might be able to financially support us again, if ever. But he was our friend, and we weren't going to walk away from this relationship. So he and I continued meeting periodically as we had done for many years.

During one lunch at Panera Bread, another donor noticed us. He was aware of the man's bankruptcy and inability to continue financially supporting ministries. Later, the donor told me how much it meant to see us sharing a meal with no strings attached.

He commented, "I always wondered what would happen if I would stop funding you. Would our relationship continue? Seeing you continue in that relationship answered that question."

For a Kingdom-focused fundraiser, the pinnacle of the relationship is not when a donation is made. Real relationships are long-term.

DISCUSSION QUESTIONS

- What are you doing today that will help establish long-term relationships with supporters?

- Do you continue in relationship even if funding ends?

9

GRATEFUL, NOT ENTITLED

Gratitude is not only the greatest of virtues, but the parent of all others.

—Cicero

After graduating from college, my friend Katie Nienow landed an internship with Young Life and began working in ministry stateside. Meanwhile, a friend of hers accepted a position with International Justice Mission, a faith-based anti-trafficking organization.

When Katie sliced open an envelope containing her friend's support letter for an upcoming trip to India, she instantly felt grateful for the opportunity to give, but didn't feel like she had the money to participate at that exact moment.

Not taking immediate action, she put the support letter aside for a few weeks. When she came across it at a later time, Katie was once again drawn to the mission of freeing slaves in the name of the Lord.

Her desire to contribute was twofold.

"This was quite clearly a response to the call of the Lord on our lives to give," Katie explained. "But it was also a chance for me to participate in something I would likely never do."

When Katie called her friend to excitedly offer support, her thankful friend explained that the expenses had already been covered.

"I remember feeling crushed that she'd raised enough before I had the chance to participate," said Katie. "In some real, tangible way, I felt like I'd missed out."

For the first time, Katie began to understand the difference between asking people for money and offering someone an opportunity to partner together. This experience caused Katie to approach all fundraising as an *offer*, not an *ask*.

Later, Katie took a fundraising position and shared the impact of this story. "I started to believe that there were many people, when I was fundraising, who would likewise be crushed if I got to them too late . . . after all the needs had been fulfilled."

We have an innate desire to be part of something bigger than ourselves. When fundraising is done correctly, supporters should be filled with gratitude for the incredible gift of playing a small part in expanding the Kingdom of God.

Gratitude should be a consistent theme of both the one raising the funds and the one donating generously. Ultimately, it's a privilege to use what we've been given by God to advance causes we believe in.

Deuteronomy 8:18 commands, "You shall remember the Lord your God, for it is he who gives you power to get wealth."[1]

The Psalms provide additional perspective: "The earth is the Lord's, and everything in it, the world, and all who live in it."[2]

Woven into these verses is one very important principle: Everything we have is from the Lord.

This awareness should lead us to unbounded gratefulness. But without being intentionally grateful, we often naturally digress to entitlement.

Entitled attitudes are irreconcilable with Kingdom-focused fundraising because we realize that everything we have, and every single gift, is from God. Both fundraisers and donors are able to express an attitude of gratitude when collaborating in expanding Christ's Kingdom.

As we seek out new relationships, it's important that we don't forget about all the people who have said yes already. When a donor has given, we focus on at least seven different times to thank them before even thinking of asking again. And we never want to presume that someone will give again just because they have given in the past.

Good work begins with gratitude in both the one making the gift and the one receiving it.

DISCUSSION QUESTIONS

- Have you thanked God for the gift of fundraising?

- Have you been thorough in thanking those who support the cause?

10

Represents, Not Uses

Almost every sinful action ever committed can be traced
back to a selfish motive. It is a trait we hate in each other
but justify in ourselves.

—Stephen Kendrick

Somewhere in Seattle's twisted maze of Starbucks and waterways sits
the headquarters of Amazon. Jeff Bezos, the company's founder, has
reshaped America's retail business and become one of the world's
wealthiest people.

Part of Jeff's leadership strategy has been to turn the company's
focus back toward the customer. To strengthen this mindset, he
reintroduced a company strategy that was originally pioneered by

Sears. Each time the executives of Amazon take their seats for a meeting, one empty chair is included at the table. Next to financial gurus and management experts, the chair serves as an ever-present reminder of the most important person in the meeting: the customer.

From questions like "What would the customer think about this decision?" to statements such as "If I were the customer, I'd prefer to have it done this way," the empty chair provokes discussion that is attuned to the customer's viewpoint.[1]

As organizations raise funds, we would do well to follow this practice and always keep a chair for the families served or the beneficiaries of the organization.

As we meet with supporters, it is a high privilege to tell stories of the men, women, and children we serve, and to connect supporters with remarkable people they might never have the privilege of meeting. Our conversation, in tone and content, should be done as if the people we are serving are in the room with us.

This stands in stark contrast to times and approaches that focus on the ministry or the philanthropist to the exclusion of the people served. When my wife and I went to serve in a refugee camp after a volcanic eruption that displaced 400,000 families, we were surprised to see the ensuing media frenzy and what it did to organizations.

The first "action" of most of the largest organizations was to plaster bumper stickers in the refugee camps. Tacking logos on telephone poles and cars, the nongovernment agencies (NGOs) marketed their image with New York ad agency efficiency. But somehow, it seemed, they forgot about the people.

Consider the blankets.

Even though we were in central Africa, the rainy season and elevation caused the weather to be surprisingly cold. People living in poverty—who were forced to leave their homes—needed warmer clothes. Between the unrelenting rain and constant chill, I was uncomfortable in my raincoat, long-sleeve shirt, and khakis. A lot of kids wore nothing but ripped T-shirts. And we had blankets to give—generously funded by churches in the U.S. and purchased locally. But we were unable to give them away.

The high-profile NGOs decided how and to whom goods and services were to be provided. Supposedly an American news crew would be following the story of a bundle of blankets arriving in Goma from the U.S. Each NGO wanted the spotlight; the leaders began debating who would give the blankets while being filmed.

Blankets were piled in our van, ready to go. Yet the refugees went without blankets for two days. Until the next shipment arrived, no blankets would be given.

When the delivery finally came, there was no CNN news crew. It had been a rumor.

Because we were no longer competing for media coverage, the larger NGOs finally granted permission for us to distribute the blankets.[2]

This sort of self-centered service uses the people served for our own purposes and undermines the credibility of our mission.

And it's not just the families served who are impacted. Ultimately, Kingdom fundraising is not just representing those we serve; we are representing our Savior. The very process of fundraising is an opportunity to develop lasting relationships through which God is working. It's an opportunity to grow in generosity and the grace of our Lord Jesus Christ. It's an opportunity to invite friends into something significant and much bigger than ourselves.

When done properly, Kingdom fundraising should result in impact, friendship, and gratitude.

DISCUSSION QUESTIONS

- Have you ever focused more on the donors than on the people served?

- Ask yourself if the supporter's life will improve by giving to your organization and if the world will be a better place by this interaction.

PART II

THE
GIVER

DAVID WEEKLEY

At twenty-three years old, I started a homebuilding business with my brother. By the time I'd turned thirty, our success had skyrocketed.

Thanks to a strong work ethic, a fear of failure, and a booming housing industry (in the late 1970s, you could fall off a truck and sell a home), we were successful beyond our wildest dreams.

Just seven years after we began, we were building over three hundred homes a year, and I got to stand up on stage once a month and talk to hundreds of industry leaders. Becoming the youngest president of the Greater Houston Builders Association, I was a presence in the homebuilding community. My involvement expanded beyond homebuilding as I also became the youngest member of the Houston Young Presidents' Organization, a network of young chief executives and business leaders around the world. All this visibility and success continued to increase my self-image and hubris.

Enjoying success, I began to build my family a 10,000-square-foot home in a prestigious Houston neighborhood. Bonnie was my high school sweetheart, and we were now able to enjoy the very best that the world had to offer. I had more money coming in than I knew how to handle. With my climbing status and newly acquired BMW, I had arrived. At the ripe age of thirty, I believed I had all the answers. I was on top of the world.

Amid this early success, I wasn't a bad guy. In keeping with my Christian upbringing, I tithed to the church and did good deeds as I was able. But I wasn't really committed to the Lord. I thought that it was all about me and my success. Thankfully, God decided to wake me up from my comfortable cultural Christianity.

My wake-up call came in the mid-1980s as the market nose-dived. In six months, new home sales in Houston plummeted from 30,000 to 6,000. We lost a crippling portion of our business. The only way we survived was by expanding to other markets to offset our losses in Houston, so I hit the road traveling to Dallas and Austin most days to ensure our survival.

I had to sell the house and the BMW. Everything I thought was important was suddenly gone.

It was as if God was telling me, "You might think you're hot stuff, and you might have done well in business, but you are *not* in control."

Looking back on those early days of success, it's hard to believe that I once had millions of dollars flowing through my hands, and literally no good came out of it. I had done little for those in need and society in general. What had I done in response to God's extraordinary blessing?

Not much.

Much of Houston felt the shock of the economic downturn. I remember seeing a bumper sticker that read, "Lord, give me one more boom, and I won't screw the next one up." That became my prayer.

I've heard people say that you shouldn't make deals with God, but I'm afraid I did. Secretly but sincerely, I promised, "If I get another opportunity, I'll do better next time." I promised God that if He blessed my business again, I would give a lot of my resources back to Him.

Turns out, I did get another opportunity. Business came back after a number of challenging years. And I did not forget what it felt like to blow my first opportunity—nor did I forget my prayer.

Earlier in my career, I had attended a mayor's prayer breakfast, and I heard businessman Stanley Tam speak. He wrote a book called *God Owns My Business,* in which he described how he set up his business so half of his earnings went directly to Kingdom endeavors.

Moved by his example, I felt called to give away half of my wealth. So in 1992, I promised, "From this point forward, I'm going to give 50 percent of my income—as well as 50 percent of my time and talents—for Kingdom endeavors."

Making that commitment was just the beginning. To actually do this, I needed to hire someone to lead the company, because it would be impossible to truly run a large, multi-market company with only 50 percent of my time.

I hired a Chief Operating Officer who later became president. Now the CEO of the company, he has led the business to even greater success. God blessed this move; He brought me someone with greater skills than I had in running a large organization. We needed a transition from entrepreneur to professional manager, but that only became clear later.

My new commitment led me to move from a "me-orientation" to an "others-orientation." The team's well-being began to take priority over profits. This time, I understood that the business wasn't all about me, a realization that many entrepreneurs never come to.

We created profit sharing, hired chaplains in all of our markets, increased the 401(k) plan, sold stock in the company to senior leaders, and carried out many other decisions that changed the entire flavor of who we were as a company. These changes simply never would have happened under the leadership of the "cultural Christian" David Weekley.

As a result, we've been named one of *Fortune* magazine's "100 Best Companies to Work For" nine times. People notice a difference in a company that treats its employees with dignity. The more I have focused on the "other" rather than myself, the more worldly success I have enjoyed, and the more Kingdom focused I have become!

I've come to believe that God wants me to use the skills and everything He's given me to do good, to love others, and to assist worthy nonprofit organizations.

Since 1992, I have had the tremendous privilege of rolling up my sleeves and engaging in active philanthropy. And I feel God's pleasure in it. There is nothing that brings more joy than using my God-given skills and resources to further Kingdom-building endeavors.

Using my business experience, I have been able to strategize and plan with nonprofit leaders so that we can dramatically scale many organizations and serve even more people well. When I travel internationally with social entrepreneurs and ministry leaders to meet individuals who have greatly improved their lives, I feel increasingly alive and "in the zone." When I serve in this way, I feel like I'm where God created me to be.

No longer do I feel guilty for what I've been given; rather, I feel incredible gratitude that I am able to serve and give. Out of that gratitude comes a deep sense of responsibility to use what has been entrusted to me in ways that honor the Giver of all gifts. When I act on that responsibility and give freely of my time, talent, and resources, I feel an awesome *joy*.

Taking my role of stewardship seriously, I want to excel in how I give. This book contains some of the key lessons I've learned about thoughtful and engaged Kingdom philanthropy. I hope they are a help to you as you discover not just happiness, but also incredible joy as you use all you've been given in service to God.

11

STEWARDSHIP, NOT OWNERSHIP

> Do you not know that God entrusted you with that
> money . . . to feed the hungry, to clothe the naked, to
> help the stranger, the widow, the fatherless; and indeed
> as far as it will go, to relieve the wants of all mankind?
> How can you, how dare you, defraud the Lord by ap-
> plying it to any other purpose?
>
> —John Wesley

The temptation always exists for us to view what we have—our
income, time, gifts, and belongings—as our own. I especially
struggled with this early on in my life, as I accumulated wealth

and allowed myself to believe that my success was due solely to my own personal strengths and talents. I rarely thought about how not only my money but also my very strengths and talents had come from God.

Fortunately, God graciously brought humility through a holy two-by-four across the forehead in Houston's housing crisis. I awoke to see that Scripture poses an alternative perspective to my philosophy of self-sufficiency: the Lord as source of all.

Deuteronomy 8:17–18 says, "Beware lest you say in your heart, 'My power and the might of my hand have gotten me this wealth.' You shall remember the Lord your God, for it is he who gives you power to get wealth."[1] I find comfort in knowing that even Israel—God's chosen people, who had experienced His provision and power firsthand—needed to be reminded not to take the credit for what they had accomplished.

The concept of Christian stewardship begins with the understanding that everything we have, all of who we are, comes from God. If that's the case, then it becomes imperative for donors to be in communication with God to determine how to use the resources entrusted to us.

There is no single formula for what stewardship looks like. But reading through Scripture, we see broad themes revealing that a primary responsibility is to give back to our neighbors in ways that are pleasing to God. I think of the story of the Good Samaritan in the gospel of Luke, a parable that challenges us to expand our definition of who our neighbor is as well as how we serve them. In this account, the Good Samaritan uses his wealth to serve someone who was, according to the culture of the day, an enemy. Despite this, the Samaritan not only cared for the person's physical needs but, more broadly, was a neighbor who "showed mercy."[2]

The beautiful thing is that we each are unique, special, and one of a kind as God made us and have the ability to positively affect this world with our time and talents, as well as with our financial resources. I have decided to give where I believe God's heart is . . . to help the poor, the lost, the disenfranchised, so that they can become the people God intends for them to be. As Romans 12:4, 6 says, "For as in one body we have many members, and the members do not all have the same function. . . . Having gifts that differ according to the grace given to us, let us use them."[3]

When we use our gifts to serve God and others for the Kingdom, we release our claim on what we have received and invite the Holy Spirit to work through us. And in my experience, this leads to true joy.

DISCUSSION QUESTIONS

- When have you taken credit for what God has given you?

- Have you ever had your own wake-up moment?

- How can we practically remember that everything we have is a gift?

12

HEADS,
NOT JUST HEARTS

A body of men, holding themselves accountable to no-
body, ought not to be trusted by anybody.

—Thomas Paine

In a free-market society, businesses prosper or decline based upon
their ability to meet customers' needs by delivering products or
services to the marketplace in a cost-effective manner.

However, this same standard is rarely held for the nonprofit sector. The economics of the nonprofit sector are often less rational
than those of the private sector, and at times there appears to be
little correlation between a nonprofit's performance and how much
donors will give them.

Most people would not make personal portfolio investment decisions without first evaluating the performance of the companies or funds in which they are investing. Yet many individuals invest significant amounts of God's financial resources in nonprofit organizations without the same kind of scrutiny. If we have been entrusted with God's resources, how can we not take seriously the stewardship of these resources?

Donors are often guilty of letting themselves be controlled by their hearts rather than their heads. As some in philanthropy remind us, "People give to people, not organizations." Philanthropic decisions are often made based upon our friendships or the interests of others we know, rather than upon our own personal investigation of the organizations seeking our support.

We can do better.

While it's certainly important to engage your heart in giving, it's equally as important to use your head. Don't let relationships or appeals to emotions cloud your judgment. Take the time to carefully investigate how to give in a way that stewards God's resources well.

Choosing where to invest resources takes a lot of work, but it's crucial that we give to organizations that will use our gifts wisely. There are currently more than 1.5 million nonprofit organizations registered in the U.S.,[1] and there are simply not enough generous donors to fully support all of them. If we allocate funds to those performing poorly, we inherently take away resources from those that perform well.

When I need to make choices about how to invest the gifts that have been entrusted to me, I start by considering two important questions. The first is driven by my heart: What do I feel called to get engaged in? The second relates to my head: How can I best advance God's Kingdom through effective stewardship of my time, talents, and resources?

Personally, I find myself called to organizations that are on the smaller side, that don't necessarily have it all figured out yet. When I committed 50 percent of my time to Kingdom endeavors, I was freed up to offer my business experience to guide the financials, board development, scaling, and so on of these growing organizations. While I usually have little to add in terms of their programing or ministry, I greatly enjoy contributing to the business aspects of their organization's health.

I have developed a set of criteria to determine if I am willing to give to a particular organization. Before I give, I try to ensure that a particular organization has:

1. A unique and well-defined mission
2. Excellent programs or services that clearly advance the mission
3. A clear way to measure results
4. A three- to five-year strategic plan
5. A business model and cost structure demonstrating that the organization will make a greater impact in a more efficient way as it grows
6. Strong executive talent
7. A strong and effective board of directors

If some of the above are missing—and with young organizations, they often are—I work with the leadership to build capacity and develop these aspects for the health of the organization.

It's also important that the organization has clear reporting for how they use donations. All too often, nonprofits claim success merely because they exist and have a compelling mission. They seek funding from donors without reporting clear and measurable results. Because nonprofits operate without the discipline of the marketplace, it is critical that donors ensure real results and the efficacy of the organization. Nonprofit organizations should be responsible for reporting back to donors how their money was spent. Because they are entrusted with gifts provided by donors, they should hold themselves to a higher standard of performance and accountability. This is especially true for faith-based nonprofits that recognize their resources as belonging to God, not to themselves.

DISCUSSION QUESTIONS

- How do you determine where you give your resources?

- Do you follow up with the organization to find out how your money was spent?

- Do you measure the efficacy of your donations as "God's investment manager"?

13

MISSION MINDED, NOT MANIPULATIVE

Remember there's no such thing as a small act of kindness. Every act creates a ripple with no logical end.

—Scott Adams

Donors are sometimes able to not only contribute to an organization financially, but also to observe its functions and provide input on its direction. When presented with this unique opportunity, donors are able to lend rare perspective as outsiders with often different skills and life experience than the organization's leaders.

For employees of a nonprofit, immediate needs can obscure long-term vision or root causes behind problems. With outside eyes, a donor is able to take in a 30,000-foot view of the organization, a new perspective that might reveal unexpected needs or innovative solutions.

For example, an organization came to me looking for a substantial gift to their main office to fund their expansion into several different cities across the nation. I was able to illustrate the experiences of many nationally known organizations that have local boards and leadership, demonstrating that most giving is locally focused. The organization adjusted their original plans and have now grown successfully from three struggling markets to twelve healthy regions. My twenty years of experience (and mistakes!) in the business world allowed me to share this knowledge with them. Of course, it all depends on whether an organization's leadership is receptive and effective, and in this case, they were.

However, the donor must also be careful not to manipulate an organization's mission to meet his or her own priorities. When a donor has strong interests, it's easy for the nonprofit to fall prey to mission drift and pander to a donor. It's certainly no easy task for an organization to balance its desire to please the donor and demonstrate effectiveness. Much of the responsibility to protect the organization's mission lies with the donor.

In a presentation, a nonprofit mentioned an idea that I was passionate about. Though the plan had not been well thought-out, I funded the idea and held the nonprofit to their unrealistic metrics. Hurting their overall performance, this situation also damaged our relationship. It would have been better for them, and me, if they had simply and honestly said they were not ready to tackle that initiative.

While an outside perspective can be extremely beneficial to an organization, it can also become distracting. It's important to keep in mind that the immediate goal is to multiply what an organization is already doing well and to remember that we all have the same ultimate goal—spreading Christ around the world.

DISCUSSION QUESTIONS

- What gifts or talents do you have that could multiply the impact of an organization that you support?

- How do you check your motives to make sure you're not unconsciously nudging an organization away from its mission?

14

PARTNERSHIP, NOT DEPENDENCY

It takes two flints to make a fire.

—Louisa May Alcott

When a donor provides support year after year, it's easy for an organization to become dependent on their support. However, an organization cannot thrive when it is dependent on the fluctuations in the hearts, minds, and wallets of donors. We have all heard the ancient proverb that tells us, "If you give a man a fish, he will eat for a day. If you teach a man to fish, he will eat for a lifetime." Rather than doling out fish to nonprofits, donors should seek to walk alongside nonprofits, partnering with them as they fish.

I usually make larger gifts to build capacity in a nonprofit—their reach, scale, growth plan, or facilities. I have found that it is not as effective to make large, ongoing operating gifts. I usually will limit an operating gift to no more than 5 percent of an organization's annual budget, and a capital gift to no more than 20 percent of the capital needed. Of course, I can point to a number of examples where I broke my own rules based upon a particular need.

It is damaging to give a handout rather than a "hand up"; we shouldn't throw money at nonprofits without helping them to perform more effectively. Instead of developing an unhealthy dependency, the partnership should become one that is mutually beneficial.

Strong Kingdom donors, especially those with some position of power and maturity, should appreciate honest and transparent communications. It is often hard for a nonprofit to tell a donor no—yet sometimes that is exactly what they should do. I appreciate a nonprofit that tells me no if they can't execute a particular idea or expansion that I suggest. They are being true to themselves, and it makes me more likely to fund them in the future.

On the other end of the spectrum, it's really easy for a donor to become demanding. While we should have high standards for how nonprofits steward our money, we must have grace for imperfections. There is no way that those of us in the marketplace can understand the challenges the leaders of nonprofit organizations face and the pressures they feel to raise funds to support their passions. So it takes a balance of transparency and honesty, respect and responsibility. When Peter had to report HOPE's struggles in the Congo, responding with condemnation would only have further slowed down the Kingdom work that HOPE does. I always appreciate transparency and honesty, as we all make mistakes, personally and in business. It is unreasonable to think a nonprofit won't have miscues. In fact, if year after year a nonprofit tells me all is great, no problems, I begin to wonder if I am getting the full story.

DISCUSSION QUESTIONS

- How do you see the concept of a "hand up" playing itself out in the organizations that you serve?

- Where could you give more grace for mistakes?

- Where might there be a lack of honesty and transparency?

15

TRANSFORMATIONAL GIVING, NOT JUST INFORMED PHILANTHROPY

It's not how much we give but how much love we put into giving.

—Mother Teresa

What if you were able to see a way to have a dramatic impact on an organization through your stewardship of resources and relationships? What if you share this with the organization's leadership and you work together to come up with a plan to improve and expand the programs and ministry? This can lead to transformational giving.

When donors share time, talent, and treasure with a nonprofit, we open up the possibility for transformation—of the organization, of the cause, and of ourselves.

Transformational giving can occur when an organization has every element in place for positive growth and change—clear goals, a compelling mission, adequate staff and infrastructure, wise visionary leadership, strong communication, established procedures for accountability and reporting—everything except the necessary funding to take action. The organization should be prepared to show donors how a substantial gift could be truly transformational to the organization—and eager to be held accountable for results. Thus, ideally, a donor's investment serves as a catalyst for the nonprofit's pre-existing plans to become reality.

Unfortunately, many nonprofits do not invest the time, energy, and resources to ensure that all of these elements are in place before approaching donors for support. As a result, the impact of a gift is blunted, or with an astute donor, the gift may never be made.

But when interaction and accountability are made possible through the initiative of the organization, excellence may be achieved. This is giving at its best, when a true partnership develops between the organization and the donor, with the organization's mission cementing the two.

I remember a large capital campaign for a new building for an organization. While this group was terrific at their programs, they were inexperienced at building. Though they got pro bono architectural help, the architect's experience was largely in retail spaces, a different animal than the low-cost warehouse and office space this organization needed. Their original plans and estimates were $200 per square foot, but as a builder, I knew their plan could be accomplished for $100 per square foot. I offered a substantial donation if they were willing to start anew, work with experienced commercial contractors, and design to a budget rather than a wish list—just like we do with our for-profit business or as homeowners. It was their choice, but they were short of funds. I agreed to fund the right architect, and they ended up getting what they needed for a price they could afford, without taking on any debt. Recruiting folks with the proper expertise can make an enormous difference.

When nonprofits ask donors for financial backing to pursue their goals, the focus is often on the change that the organization or cause will experience. But we, as donors, also frequently experience transformation as a result of our involvement.

Bill Ackman, founder and CEO of a hedge fund management company and a member of the Giving Pledge, has written, "The happiness and optimism I have obtained from helping others are a big part of what keeps me sane."[1]

As donors, perhaps we need to be asking not just, "Will giving to this nonprofit or cause bring about transformation?" but also, "Will giving to this nonprofit or cause transform *me*? Should I consider this opportunity to give because I need to change some area of my life? Maybe I simply need to hold God's resources loosely and start counting how much I have given away, rather than what I have accumulated."

At its core, giving is a spiritual exercise that demands us to reckon with where we truly place our hope—whether we're trusting in our own provision or in God's. Paul writes about this in 1 Timothy 6:17–19:

> Command those who are rich in this present world not to be arrogant nor to put their hope in wealth, which is so uncertain, but to put their hope in God, who richly provides us with everything for our

enjoyment. Command them to do good, to be rich in good deeds, and to be generous and willing to share. In this way they will lay up treasure for themselves as a firm foundation for the coming age, so that they may take hold of the life that is truly life.

Giving is a mutually transformative experience, a call to growth, faith, and learning for everyone involved. We are to exercise good stewardship with the utmost care, creativity, and joy!

DISCUSSION QUESTIONS

- How have you experienced transformative giving?

- What opportunities could you seek out that could not only make a difference in the world but also transform your own heart?

16

SPIRIT-LED, NOT OVERLY STRUCTURED

Earthly wisdom is doing what comes naturally. Godly
wisdom is doing what the Holy Spirit compels us to do.

—Charles Stanley

Several years ago, I was sitting in my office when my phone rang.
It was Anthony, the director of a Christian camp in the area. He
proceeded to tell me that he had a significant amount of debt on his
camp, and the bank was planning to shut it down if they couldn't
pay within sixty days.

This is usually the kind of situation that I avoid. I am passionate about the impact that Christian camps can have on kids, but
I've found that giving to desperate situations rarely works out. Yet

something urged me to consider this as an opportunity. As Anthony spoke, I felt the Spirit nudging me to reconsider and engage in the situation.

I reached out to two of my friends who are also passionate about Christian youth camps. We asked Anthony to send us a lot of information. After reviewing it and ascertaining if it was a good camp, we asked him to meet with us. After deliberating the most effective way to support Anthony's camp, we paid off the camp's debt and re-crafted their board of directors. Today, the camp is thriving financially and touches 15,000 kids each year—10,000 more than when Anthony called. God certainly rewarded our open-mindedness and risk taking to keep this camp operational.

As I give, I try to remain sensitive to where the Holy Spirit is moving. There have been three or four times in the last ten years when I have thrown my rules, metrics, and deep analysis out the window because I had a strong sense that this was something I needed to do. Every time I've acted on that prompting from the Spirit, the results for the Kingdom have been spectacular.

Biblically, we see God leading people to invest deeply in projects that seemed destined to fail. God instructed the Israelites to march around Jericho to knock down the walls of the city.[1] When Gideon was about to take his army to fight the Midianites, God whittled his army down from 32,000 to just 300 men.[2] Elijah drenched his altar with water while praying for God to set the altar on fire.[3] And every time, God proved himself faithful.

As important as it is to give with your brain engaged, it's equally important to be willing to sacrifice your standard processes if the Holy Spirit leads. Recognize that God can lead in ways that don't follow your format, and be willing to follow Him any way He leads. Prayer is therefore essential in the giving process, as is taking time to reflect. I am by nature fast and reactionary and have learned from friends to pause, pray, reflect, and listen to God's promptings—and then decisions seem clearer.

DISCUSSION QUESTIONS

- Do you pray before giving?

- How do you make sure you're being sensitive to the Holy Spirit's leading?

- How do you balance prudence with a willingness to obey God?

17

ANONYMOUS
OR NAMED?

But when you give to the needy, do not let your left hand
know what your right hand is doing.

—Matthew 6:3

As executor of my parents' estate, I recently named a building in
their honor. The building was in a prominent location, and it quickly
became known by our family name. But in reality, my parents had
not had any significant involvement with the organization in many
years. The recognition that they (and I) were getting was totally inap-
propriate for our level of involvement. To make matters worse, my
parents were very humble people who didn't like a lot of recognition
for their contributions.

I finally had to realize that, while I had thought I had good intentions, the decision was more about me than them. I have since asked the organization to remove their name and give the recognition to one of the founders or someone who was involved in a more significant way than simply writing a check. Now I can feel my parents smiling down from above rather than grimacing.

It's always a tough dilemma for me when organizations want to honor a donor with a "named" room, building, or scholarship. For many, the dilemma is on a smaller scale, but the dilemma is the same. Often, universities or nonprofits will ask donors if they can list their names in a newsletter after they've given. Is it wrong to agree? As a believer, how am I to react to these scenarios? If our Creator is the giver of wealth, then why should my family or I get the credit? Yet, honestly, my ego likes to have my name on things. Deep down, I like the idea of adding to my legacy.

Also, there are some arguments that giving publicly actually benefits the nonprofit sector. Patricia Illingworth, professor of philosophy at Northeastern University, said, "Public giving is more desirable in many ways, because it really creates this culture of giving."[1] People are often inspired to give to an organization when someone they respect gives to them. So then, maybe I am not being boastful if I tell my friends about incredible organizations that I support?

As with so many things in the Christian faith, it comes down to motivation. There are selfish reasons to go public and to be anonymous. Some donors attempt to seal their immortality by slapping their names on buildings; others remain anonymous to avoid being harassed for money by other organizations. The real question is not, Should I give anonymously? The question is, How will I gain the most glory for God?

I have recently begun the practice of accepting the naming rights, but naming the conference room or chapel something like "Grace Chapel" rather than the "Weekley Chapel." This allows me to glorify God and gain a small sense of inward affirmation.

DISCUSSION QUESTIONS

- Examine the motivations behind your giving habits in the past. Are you seeking to gain the glory for God first and foremost?

18

THE KIDS
OR THE KINGDOM?

I knew I didn't think it was a good idea to give the
money to my kids. That wouldn't be good either for
my kids or society.

—Bill Gates

All wealthy Americans (and, by worldly standards, most Americans
fall into that category) have to figure out how money should impact
our children. Is it to be used to ensure that our kids don't have to
work as hard as we did? To give them a leg up? Or to simply allow
them to live off our gifts?

Many are now realizing that wealth can be a crippling gift to a
younger generation—sapping motivation, limiting vision, decreasing

confidence, and eroding drive. Andrew Carnegie famously coined the phrase, "Shirtsleeves to shirtsleeves in three generations," meaning that the descendants of successful people are likely to misuse their wealth. When children are handed everything on a silver platter, they don't have to learn how to work, to motivate themselves, to survive.[1] In our attempts to provide the best for our children, we often harm them.

If your wealth was indeed given to *you* by God, isn't it *you* who should invest it on His behalf (be it in Kingdom work, your favorite local charity, your kids, etc.)? We should not shirk our responsibility to make definitive decisions about what to do with what we have been given. We can and should make operative decisions while we are living regarding our resources, our children, and our communities. If we don't, it can often create family grief and consternation after we are gone. As parents, this is our duty.

The question is usually not whether to give the kids anything or not, as most of us do want to leave a legacy of some sort to our children. The issue is how much to leave to the kids and how and when to have it impact their lives.

One of my worst nightmares would be to have my financial blessings become a curse to my children by taking away motivation or tempting them to put their trust in something besides the Lord. I believe we all have a purpose in life, and we feel God's presence when we are using the skills and talents He gave us in service of others. If our material resources make our children more worldly and materialistic, then we have done them harm. That's the last thing any of us would want for our kids.

This is one of the toughest questions that many well-resourced families have to deal with, and there is no perfect answer. The reality is that children learn how to interact with money and giving or getting at an early age by observing their parents. Do they see you very interested in the car you drive or what you wear—or do they see parents who put money in the offering plate every weekend (as I saw my dad do)? Do they think about those less fortunate? This is what really sets kids' values, not simply whether they get a little or a lot. In fact, many of our kids have greater skills and passion for the world than we ever did. Maybe the question should be, How can we best help them live out their purpose and dreams?

DISCUSSION QUESTIONS

- How do you determine how to handle money with your children?

- What are you modeling for them when it comes to money?

- Are you teaching them financial literacy, giving, and stewardship?

19

FOR FOREVER
OR FOR NOW?

Real generosity toward the future lies in giving all to
the present.

—Albert Camus

Should our goal be to create a foundation that lives forever, carries
our name, and builds for generations (and is therefore not currently
being significantly distributed)? Not in my view. Again, for some
reason, God gifted each of us with certain skills, talents, and wealth,
and I believe they are to be used to expand the Kingdom *today*, not
to be held for future needs or generations. We have no idea about
the beliefs, needs, or desires of future generations. But we *do* know
our own God-given beliefs, experiences, and feelings *today*. Let us

use the funds now, rather than holding them for an unknown giver and belief system in the future. They were given to us, and I believe it is our responsibility as stewards to use them *now*.

In exploring the lives and legacies of previous philanthropists, I've discovered the seeming inevitability of drift. The founder's passion seems to seldom be successfully transferred to future generations. Pew Charitable Trusts is a clear example of this. Howard Pew, founder of Sun Oil (later known as Sunoco), was a passionate follower of Jesus who provided the seed capital for *Christianity Today* and Gordon Conwell Theological Seminary, among many other causes. Yet today, the Trust that bears his name provides support to organizations that clearly would not have fit his beliefs and passions.

The drift has been so marked that one author describes it as "the gravest violation of donor intent."[1] In other words, the Pew Charitable Trusts haven't done what Howard Pew founded them to do. In many ways, they've taken a full U-turn from the work Howard Pew believed in. Journalist Lucinda Fleeson aptly described the complete reversal of Howard Pew's intentions:

> [Howard] Pew couldn't find any seminary conservative enough . . . so he built his own. In 1970, he bought a 100-acre former Carmelite monastery near Boston and created the Gordon-Conwell Theological Seminary to turn out the type of ministers he sought. He built much of the campus and promised yearly checks to keep it operating. Today, the Pew Charitable Trusts give millions of dollars to Princeton University and other Ivy League colleges. They have cut off the annual funding to the Gordon-Conwell seminary.[2]

Simply stated, I don't want that to happen to the resources God has entrusted to me. So as much as possible, I want to be directly involved in investing today in causes that I care deeply about. Since none of us know the time of our death, I want to invest God's resources freely now. I have outlined several areas of giving where I would like my resources to go after my death. And I have set a twenty-five-year spend-down policy for my foundation so people who know my beliefs and giving focus are the ones to spend down the rest after I am gone.

DISCUSSION QUESTIONS

- How do you react to the responsibility of the resources that God has entrusted you with?

- How does it prompt you to use your resources today?

20

Together,
Not Alone

Let us consider how we may spur one another on toward
love and good deeds.

—Hebrews 10:24

As an entrepreneur and organizational leader from a young age, I've
faced loneliness many times. Even with my closest friends and family,
I've found it tough to admit insecurity and weakness, or to ask for help.

Looking for community, I joined the Young Presidents' Organization in my late twenties and was able to gain wisdom from
seasoned business professionals who had been through many similar
challenges and successfully navigated leadership pain points. Yet by
my early forties, this secular group made me long for a group where
faith was a centerpiece of our conversations. At this point, I was

fully convinced that I had a higher purpose on this earth than just becoming increasingly self-indulgent.

Serving on several boards of Christian ministries, I realized that there was a distinctiveness to these fellow Christian board members. Many believed in performance and accountability for ministries as I did. But meeting many Spirit-filled entrepreneurs who ran their own businesses, I saw how they incorporated their faith into how they led. Many of these individuals, met through service opportunities, have become my closest friends.

Beyond business advice, I've been inspired by their example of generosity and have been challenged to grow in my giving. For too long, the majority of my giving was done independently and without community. But that began to change as I served on a regional Young Life board in the mid 1990s. Believing in this ministry model, several of us wanted the organization to reach more kids, and we started challenging them to grow. And grow they did!

We discovered that when we pooled our giving, we could get more accomplished. Additionally, when we shared our different perspectives on important issues, we usually came up with better solutions than any one of us would have alone.

Two decades later, we are still bound together in our friendship and in our giving. We discovered immense joy in working together and tackling larger opportunities than we ever could have tackled alone. Giving, no matter what the level, is a whole lot more enjoyable when done in community and with friends.

Seeing the power of community, we've created a group to strategically give internationally. Because of the pooled resources, we have the opportunity to meet with ministry leaders and tackle larger issues than we could alone. We learn together, hear different points of view, and argue good-naturedly about which paths to take.

Giving in community always seems to result in a greater impact and in better decisions. We are peers, trying to do the right thing for the Kingdom, with no other conflicting agendas. This is so refreshing in our world of self-interest and personal aggrandizement.

Our goal in these giving groups is, as the author of Hebrews writes, to "spur one another on toward love and good deeds."[1] My friends have been a source of accountability and encouragement and have helped me resist the constant temptation to slip into materialism. We need friends to help us avoid the lure of materialism as society celebrates what we have accumulated, not what we give away, directly in opposition to Jesus' teaching that it is "more blessed to give than to receive."[2]

Over the past decades, I have been truly blessed to stand with my "Band of Brothers"—men dedicated to Kingdom endeavors who acknowledge that all we have belongs to God and that one of our roles on this earth is to determine how to best invest God's money. We argue, cajole, challenge, and pray with one another. Scripture reminds us that "iron sharpens iron,"[3] and we've found this to be true. This group of like-minded, selfless givers whom I look up to and learn from is one of life's special blessings for me.

My prayer would be that you could find and cultivate your own "Band of Brothers" and experience the joy of community in your giving.

DISCUSSION QUESTIONS

- Do you have a group of people with shared Christian interests who will challenge you?

- Do you stop and listen to the views of others as they invariably see problems with a different lens than you do?

CONCLUSION

PETER GREER & DAVID WEEKLEY

Driving along potholed roads in remote Rwanda, we reached a rural community and entered a small church with a dirt floor. Inside was a vibrant group of thirty women. With only one drum, they sang and danced—and we did our best to awkwardly clap along.

As the women went through the regular business meeting of a savings group through the local church, we were impressed by their organization, drive, and care for one another. Their prayers were passionate—and we were touched to hear them pray for us as well. Sharing stories of how they had invested in one another's businesses, this was a remarkable group of Kingdom entrepreneurs.

But it wasn't just that this was a savings group in rural Rwanda that impacted us—it was that these women were each battling HIV/AIDS. As they grew their businesses, they were also pooling their savings and covering all of the funeral expenses when one of their members died. Knowing that funeral expenses can trap a family in debt and poverty, they were determined to provide for one another.

It was their love, their strength and wisdom, and their faith and friendship that enabled them to walk with one another into eternity.

Having a tear or two in our eyes as we left, we were deeply impacted by their stories and their courage. And in some small way, there was joy in knowing God had allowed us to play a small part in this group.

David funded this program, HOPE provided the training and equipped the local team, the women contributed their strength and compassion, and the local church provided the connections behind this moment.

This was a small picture of Kingdom fundraising. We're all a part of this mission.

We're all giving and we're all receiving, collectively doing something far greater than any one person could do alone. And our lives, and the lives of many others, are being impacted. It should be a source of great joy, not obligation or drudgery, to be engaged in loving God and loving our neighbors.

May a flood of Kingdom generosity begin in and flow through each of us!

Acknowledgments

This book would not have happened without the incredible inspiration and support given to us by friends and family. Special thanks to Terry Looper, Rusty Walter, Jeff Hildebrand, John Montgomery, Wil VanLoh, and Kevin Hunt.

Tiger Dawson has been a friend, mentor, co-conspirator in giving, and part of so many of the stories in this book.

Special thanks to Abigail Ferenczy, who graciously added this project to her intern responsibilities and was instrumental in creating the first draft.

Andy McGuire, you saw the potential for this book in a Caribou Coffee and worked hard to make it happen. Andrew Wolgemuth, thank you once again for going above and beyond as our literary agent. You both excel at what you do.

Thanks to the Bethany House team, especially Ellen Chalifoux for your expert editing and Carra Carr for helping us share about this book. From start to finish, the Bethany House team has set the standard for excellence in publishing.

Fred Smith, thank you for providing a special place for community and relationships to grow through the Gathering, in addition to generously writing our foreword.

Additional support and encouragement came from Chris Crane, Sarah Ann Schultz, Kristine Frey, Becca Wammack, Anna Haggard, Jon and Jen Greer, Kim King, Kate Berkey, Danielle Towne, Claire Stewart, Ashley Dickens, Jeff Rutt, Jeff Brown, Chris Horst, Jenn Tarbell, and Kevin Tordoff.

Thank you to the faithful supporters of HOPE International. You have walked with us in sharing the love of Christ around the world, and also shown grace when we haven't fully lived out the principles outlined in this book. We are deeply thankful to God for each of you.

We also thank our families for their extraordinary love and support through this project and through our lives. We love you!

Ultimately, we thank our Savior for providing the definitive model of grace and generosity.

DAVID WEEKLEY
FAMILY FOUNDATION'S
INTERNATIONAL
GIVING SUMMARY

Mission

> The Weekley family strives to engage the world with
> integrity, creativity, curiosity, faith, and gratitude. We
> are committed to the improvement of self, the respon-
> sibility to family, and the betterment of our community
> and the world.

In keeping with this mission, the David Weekley Family Foundation
(DWFF) was established in 1990 with profits earned from David
Weekley Homes, a homebuilding company started by David at an
early age with financing from and in partnership with his brother,
Richard Weekley. The company has been blessed over the last four
decades and has approximately $1.5 billion in revenues each year.
A significant portion of its earnings fund the foundation.

In the strong conviction that all we have—our time, talents, and resources—comes from God, we believe that we have a responsibility to give back and serve others. We are each unique in the ability to positively impact this world, and when we each use our specific gifts and resources, it leads to pure joy as we live our lives serving one another.

The David Weekley Family Foundation feels particularly called to support the work of social entrepreneurs to build innovative organizations that effectively serve the world's most materially poor people. Given David's business background and entrepreneurial gifting, DWFF is eager to assist high-impact organizations scale their operations through financial assistance and capacity building.

With great joy and admiration, we consider ourselves blessed to be able to come alongside organizations that combat extreme poverty across the globe.

Focus

High Leverage, Scalable, and Sustainable

We are a Christian faith-based foundation that impacts the world through both Christ-centered and secular organizations. In our philanthropy, we look for three fundamental principles in an organization: High Leverage—they accomplish a lot with a little. Scalable—they have the propensity to grow to impact millions of people. Sustainable—over time their model utilizes some type of self-generating revenue.

Health, Education, and Livelihoods

Our focus is on enabling the materially poor to lift themselves out of poverty. We zero in on increasing income and improving job opportunities in the majority world. With greater income, people are better able to support their families by providing food and healthcare and pursuing education. By helping organizations fulfill these basic needs with market-based solutions, we strengthen societies and develop economies.

About half of our international grantees also integrate their Christian faith into this work. While physical needs are obvious to all, we believe that people also have spiritual needs that can best be addressed by faith in God.

What We Like

Entrepreneurial Leaders

Solving the world's most pressing problems requires bold and imaginative leadership. Entrepreneurial leaders dream big and take calculated risks. They constantly defy the status quo and seek innovative solutions to complex problems. They live their lives with a sense of urgency and persistence. When they make mistakes, they learn from them and are better because of them.

Fiscal Responsibility and Measurable Results

The economics of the nonprofit sector are less rational than the private sector, and there is often little correlation between a nonprofit's execution of its mission and its ability to fund itself. We believe that biblical stewardship of God's resources demands that we use our minds as well as our hearts in deciding which nonprofits and ministries to fund. This means we ask tough questions and insist on measurable results. We work in partnership with the organizations we support to find contextually appropriate ways to measure and report progress and outcomes.

Market-Based Solutions

International development almost always has the best of intentions, but it sometimes has minimal long-term impact on the intended beneficiaries and can, in fact, have negative consequences—such as distorting natural market forces and creating long-term dependency. For these reasons, it is very rare for DWFF to support handouts. We believe that handouts promote paternalism and rob people of the God-given dignity of providing for themselves and their families.

Accordingly, we like to invest in organizations that seek to uncover and tackle real market demand in the developing world. What does a market-based mind-set look like? For some organizations, it may mean having an earned revenue stream—for example, charging reasonable fees for programs or services, or directly selling life-saving products to the materially poor.

We believe that operating in a market-sensitive way forces organizations to pay attention to their real customers, the poor, and to constantly refine their value proposition. In addition, organizations that employ market-based solutions are more likely to become sustainable in the long run because they are less reliant on outside funding.

Spiritual Integration

We cannot pretend that integrating our Christian faith with our daily work is easy, but we're excited to walk alongside organizations that try. We have found that the more we compartmentalize our faith and our work, the less genuine and robust each are. For this reason, among others, we wholeheartedly encourage our Christian brothers and sisters to run holistic programming that impacts the mind, body, and spirit. For our Christian partners, measuring spiritual impact is a tremendous challenge but a worthwhile task.

What Concerns Us

Lack of Accountability

We believe that nonprofits should hold themselves to a higher standard of performance and accountability because they are entrusted with gifts provided by donors who can freely choose to support any—or none—of the millions of charities that exist today. We hold faith-based groups to the same accountability standards in performance and stewardship as secular nonprofits because we believe that excellence in our work is firmly supported biblically.

Words Without Deeds

We place a strong emphasis on supporting Christian ministries that address spiritual and physical poverty in a balanced and integrated way. We do not fund individual missionaries or episodic evangelism. This is partly due to the realities of sharing the Gospel in the developing world; when people are hurt, hungry, or have limited access to quality education, it is difficult to embrace true spiritual transformation. We also believe that discipleship is as important as evangelism, recognizing that each of our faith journeys is a lifelong quest and that God uses the church as a tool of growth and longevity.

How We Partner

The David Weekley Family Foundation practices a venture philanthropy model of giving. This means we prefer to partner with early-stage organizations that demonstrate high potential and stand to benefit from our financial, intellectual, and human capital. We typically start to partner with organizations whose operating budgets are between $500,000 and $5,000,000, providing general operating support and occasionally low-interest loans. We prefer to make transformational gifts, which we define as injections of financial and human capital that will help an organization build its capacity to scale, reach self-sufficiency, or test innovative ideas. Venture philanthropy also means that we focus on measurable results and expect regular, transparent investor updates.

Our Strongest Partners Display the Following Traits

- A unique and well-defined mission
- Excellent programs or services that clearly advance the mission
- A clear path to measure results
- A three- to five-year strategic plan
- A business model and cost structure demonstrating that the organization will make a greater impact in a more efficient way as it grows
- Strong executive talent with a coachable spirit
- A strong and effective board of directors, or a desire to establish one
- A spiritual integration plan or willingness to create one (for our Christian partners)

Notes

Introduction

1. Psalm 81:10 KJV
2. Giving Statistics, Charity Navigator, www.charitynavigator.org/index.cfm/bay/content.view/cpid/42#.VRmaq_nF9S0.
3. Be sure to read *When Helping Hurts* by Steve Corbett and Brian Fikkert and *Toxic Charity* by Bob Lupton.
4. See Matthew 6:10.

Part I: The Gift

1. Philippians 1:5
2. Elizabeth W. Dunn, Lara B. Aknin, and Michael I. Norton, "Spending Money on Others Promotes Happiness," *Science* 319 (March 2008): 1687–1688.
3. Ibid.
4. Amanda L. Chan, "7 Science-Backed Reasons Why Generosity Is Good for Your Health," *Huffington Post*, December 1, 2013, www.huffingtonpost.com/2013/12/01/generosity-health_n_4323727.html.
5. Acts 20:35
6. Proverbs 11:25
7. Raymund Flandez, "The Cost of High Turnover in Fundraising Jobs," *The Chronicle of Philanthropy*, April 2, 2012, https://philanthropy.com/article/The-Cost-of-High-Turnover-in/226573.
8. Jeanne Bell and Marla Cornelius. "Underdeveloped: A National Study of Challenges Facing Nonprofit Fundraising," CompassPoint, 2012, http://www.compasspoint.org/sites/default/files/images/UnderDeveloped_CompassPoint_HaasJrFund_January%202013.pdf.
9. Ibid.
10. 2 Corinthians 8:7

Chapter 1: Christ-Centered, Not Me-Centered

1. John 5:19

Chapter 2: Listen First, Speak Second

1. Mortimer Adler, *How to Speak, How to Listen* (New York: Touchstone, 1983), 5.

2. Susan Young, "Infographic: Insights Into Our Communication," *Get In Front Communications*, www.getinfrontcommunications.com/infographic-insights-into-our-communication.php.

Chapter 4: Clarity, Not Ambiguity

1. "Mathematical Quotations," Furman University, http://math.furman.edu/~mwoodard/ascquotg.html.

Chapter 5: Real, Not Rose-Colored

1. 2 Corinthians 12:9, emphasis added

Chapter 7: Confident, Not Arrogant

1. The opening illustration of this chapter is taken from Peter Greer and Chris Horst, *Mission Drift* (Bloomington, MN: Bethany House, 2014), 15–16.

Chapter 9: Grateful, Not Entitled

1. ESV
2. Psalm 24:1

Chapter 10: Represents, Not Uses

1. George Anders, "Jeff Bezos's Top 10 Leadership Lessons," *Forbes*, April 4, 2012, www.forbes.com/sites/georgeanders/2012/04/04/bezos-tips.

2. The story about the blanket distribution is taken from Peter Greer, *The Spiritual Danger of Doing Good* (Bloomington, MN: Bethany House, 2013), 21–22.

Part II: The Giver

Chapter 11: Stewardship, Not Ownership

1. ESV
2. See Luke 10:37 ESV.
3. ESV

Chapter 12: Heads, Not Just Hearts

1. "Knowledge Base," Grant Space, http://grantspace.org/tools/knowledge-base/Funding-Research/Statistics/number-of-nonprofits-in-the-u.s.

Chapter 15: Transformational Giving, Not Just Informed Philanthropy

1. Bill Ackman, "Bill and Karen Ackman," Billionaire Mailing List, www.billionairemailinglist.com/Billionaires%20Bill%20and%20Karen%20Ackman%20Letter%20To%20Bill%20Gates.pdf.

Chapter 16: Spirit-Led, Not Overly Structured

1. Joshua 6
2. Judges 7
3. 1 Kings 18

Chapter 17: Anonymous or Named?

1. Mark Oppenheimer, "In Big-Dollar Philanthropy, (Your Name Here) vs. Anonymity," *The New York Times*, May 10, 2013, www.nytimes.com/2013/05/11/us/in-philanthropy-your-name-here-vs-anonymous-giving.html?pagewanted=all&_r=0.

Chapter 18: The Kids or the Kingdom?

1. Jennifer Senior, "Rich Kid Syndrome," *New York* magazine, January 7, 2008, http://nymag.com/news/features/42595.

Chapter 19: For Forever or For Now?

1. Martin Morse Wooster, *The Great Philanthropists and the Problem of "Donor Intent,"* 3rd edition (Washington, D.C.: Capital Research Center, 2007), 44.
2. Lucinda Fleeson, "How a Foundation Reinvented Itself," *The Philadelphia Inquirer*, April 27, 1992, http://articles.philly.com/1992-04-27/news/26001700_1_pew-grants-pew-officials-foundation.

Chapter 20: Together, Not Alone

1. Hebrews 10:24
2. Acts 20:35
3. Proverbs 27:17

About the Authors

Peter Greer

Peter Greer is president and CEO of HOPE International and coauthor of *Entrepreneurship for Human Flourishing, Mission Drift, The Spiritual Danger of Doing Good,* and *The Poor Will Be Glad*. Peter resides in Lancaster, Pennsylvania, with his wife, Laurel, and their three children. Learn more at www.peterkgreer.com, on Twitter (@peterkgreer), and Facebook (facebook.com/peterkgreer).

David Weekley

David Weekley is the founder of one of America's largest private homebuilding companies, ranked the #14 Best Company to Work For by *Fortune* magazine in 2015. As a community leader in Houston, Texas, David has served on over twenty local boards involved in healthcare, education, and character development. Through the David Weekley Family Foundation, he's worked closely with dozens of global non-profits, including International Justice Mission and HOPE International. In 2015, he was awarded the William E. Simon Prize by the Philanthropy Roundtable. David and Bonnie have been married since 1976, have three children and five grandchildren, and reside in Houston, Texas.

HOPE
INTERNATIONAL

More From Peter Greer

BETHANYHOUSE